Practically Perfect Puppy & Other Lies

What else didn't they tell you about getting a puppy?

Meera Jethwa

Meera Puppins Publishing

ISBN: 978-1-3999-4363-5

Contents

Here's what the people who read this book before you had to say about it

"Finally! Puppy parenting in a language everyone can understand! This book by Meera Puppins should be the first port of call for anyone thinking of getting a puppy (or adopting a rescue puppy). To prepare yourself for what lies ahead, before you are bewitched by those puppy dog eyes, and before you bring your little bundle of joy home."

— Tig Tay George, mum to Mus (known affectionately as Mus the Spanish mutt)

"This is the book to dispel many of the urban myths about puppy ownership, with emphasis on puppy behaviour, and the importance of creating a bond between puppy and owner. Having booked Meera to help with our puppy's socialisation, her approach really does make your puppy practically perfect."

— Gemma & Steve Lea, parents to Betty the Wheaten Terrier puppy and Higgs the Border Terrier

"I don't have a dog. I have three TinySheep, two cats, a corn snake, and variable numbers of chickens... but no dog. One day, though, I'd love to have a dog — and Meera is the person I'll be going to for advice. Because this book is the real deal: the good, the bad, and the terribly ugly about puppy ownership and adoption. It gently removes the rose-tinted glasses and shows you what you're in for — which is a good thing, because the end result is happier dogs, happier owners, and fewer pets in rescue centres. If you're thinking of a puppy, read this first."

— Vicky Quinn Fraser, currently dog-less but one day, who knows?

Why I wrote this book

I wrote this book because I wanted to. I love writing, and I love talking to puppy owners.

As Meera Puppins, puppy trainer and puppy socialisation expert, I was talking to lots of puppy clients about things that don't appear in traditional puppy training books. The more I talked to you, the more I listened to the problems you were having with raising, training, and socialising your puppies. The more questions you asked, the more I realised how confused you were about how to train and socialise your puppy, which methods to follow and which to ignore. So many of you were being overwhelmed by conflicting puppy training advice, which then left you feeling fed up and frustrated.

I wrote this book because you, as a puppy owner, don't need another manual on how to raise, train or socialise your puppy. You don't need more advice. Really, you don't. But you do need to be heard, to be reassured, to be understood.

You need to know that it's ok to worry that you might have made a mistake by getting a puppy (you haven't, you're just sleep deprived). You need to talk about the things that are really bothering you – and yes, it is perfectly natural to resent your puppy at times. It's also totally normal for your puppy to sometimes be the source of arguments in your otherwise happy family or personal life.

I wrote this book because I wanted to talk to you about the puppy things that no one else is talking about.

If you'd like to talk to me directly, or join in with the puppy conversation that we should be having, please get in touch with me at www.meerapuppins.co.uk/contact.

The Page I Didn't Want to Write

My lovely book coach, Vicky Quinn Fraser, asked me to write an introduction to my book.

Well, the book is finished now, but I still haven't written this page — because I don't really want to. It scares me. I want to shove this page into a darkened drawer until I forget it exists.

What if I say the wrong things?

What if you stop reading?

What if you think this page is crap, and then judge the entire book based on it?

Do you see my dilemma?

Can't we just skip this bit and get to the nitty gritty of the puppy stuff?

The answer is apparently "no."

Sorry.

So here goes.

The big idea for this book is to have the conversation that no-one else is having with you about your puppy. I want to talk to you about all the things that are being kept eerily quiet, and I want to help you navigate through the chaos, worry, and stress of raising your puppy.

But not by plying you with promises of easy-peasy training, or by stuffing you with technical information. Instead, I want to help you be confident, calm and reassured when you're raising your puppy. I'd like you to focus on building a bond with your puppy by following my signature relationship first puppy training system, which will make your training journey a lot easier.

I don't know which stage of the puppy journey you're at, but I imagine you could be getting ready to welcome your puppy.

Or perhaps your puppy is already home and you're finding things a bit "argh, I'm a puppy owner, get me out of here."

Or maybe your puppy is a bit older now, but you're curious to see what you've missed out on. Or perhaps your current dog is getting on a bit, so you're thinking about getting a puppy, but it's been a while since you had one, and you want to prepare yourself for what lies ahead.

Maybe you've rescued a puppy (rescue dogs are my favourite breed, please get in touch if this is you, I love reading rescue dog stories!) and are feeling a bit "Whoa! What the heck have we let ourselves in for?!"

Whichever stage you're at, I promise you the best. The best support, the best efforts, the best of my knowledge and advice — and my best attempt to write this book in a way that is helpful and comforting to you. As you read this book, I hope you feel supported, reassured and empowered that you absolutely do have what it takes to raise your puppy to be practically perfect (not a lie).

The best books begin with the love of a dog
and so I dedicate this book to G, and to Theo,
my very far from perfect dogs
but my perfect companions.

Wherever you both are now,
this book would never have happened without you
(and also without me, owner of opposable thumbs).

"If I told your story, where would you like me to start?"
asked the human.

"In the middle," replied the dog.
"I would like you to start in the middle."

"Why in the middle?"
wondered the human.

"Well," replied the dog,
"in the beginning, we were just a couple of strangers."

@humum_andthe_greyhound

Practically Perfect Puppy Lie Number 1

Happily Ever After

Happily ever after is a Disney-like dream when we become puppy owners. Puppies are magical creatures, and they are born with a spell-binding power to transform our dreary lives into daily adventures. When we bring our puppies home, it is with the intention of forever. Of happily ever after. We dream of our practically perfect puppies; we fantasise about raising, training and socialising them into equally perfect companions. This is often part of our holy-grail quest to achieve puppy perfection.

But it's a lie to pretend puppy ownership is a fairytale, and even less realistic to expect our puppies to behave practically perfectly all of the time. Somewhere in our puppy story, we may be faced with a vicious and unexpected villain. And that is why this book begins with the terrible truth behind a happily-ever-after ending.

On May 23rd, 2019, I was forced to say goodbye to the dog that changed my life.

Granted, nobody was holding a gun to my head (despite living in South East London at the time) nor were they physically prising her lead out of my sweaty, slightly polluted hands. Yet the decision was still forced, and I had to say goodbye.

When puppy owners share with me their heartbreaking stories of doing everything "right" for their puppies, yet things still go wrong, their stories take me back to May 23rd. They worry that their puppy's biting is a sign of aggression; they panic that they're doing things wrong despite reading books, attending puppy classes or booking a puppy trainer. They don't know how to cope if their puppy can't be left home alone.

Perhaps life throws them into less than ideal circumstances which are beyond their control. Their relationships disintegrate, their finances crumble, or debilitating illness sets in and takes a crippling hold. Their responsibilities and obligations change, their job is taken away, their landlord changes their mind, or the neighbours file a nuisance dog complaint.

Or, their puppies are attacked by another dog, causing an onslaught of behavioural problems. Sometimes, their puppies are caught up in accidents, causing them to be on rest for weeks or months, squashing every chance to raise their puppy "normally".

Sometimes, these things have happened close together in a run of terrible luck. The consequences are life-changing, and this is often when the impossible thought of ever giving up on their puppy mutates from something that only happens to other people, into a terrible, painful reality. I know this, because it happened to me too.

Before MeeraPuppins, I had a niche job as a Spanish-English translator, and I worked in-house for a Spanish bank. I was finally able and prepared to commit to the responsibilities of dog ownership, with the added flexibility of being a work-from-home dog mum. I thought I had met my life partner, with whom I could share the joys (and burdens) of being a dog-mum. We lived together in a plush rental property in a gorgeously leafy, green and dog-friendly area of London. We had the landlord's permission to get a dog, with only a couple of easy caveats. I also had an extensive and supportive network of dog-loving friends to help us out. I'm telling you this because on the face of it, I was a practically perfect dog owner: primed, primped and ready to adopt my first dog. Reality, of course, barks and bites louder and harder than you ever imagine it will.

Doing everything right, and yet things still go wrong

Just like you, I was determined to do everything right before we got our dog.

Despite my best efforts, things still went wrong. This is not uncommon – it happens more often than you might think. At some point, nearly every single one of my private puppy training or socialisation clients have shared with me how long and how extensively they prepared for the arrival of their puppy. They show me their reams of research into their chosen breed of puppy, they share stories of the breeders they vetted, the recommendations they sought, the friends they interrogated about what it's *really* like to get a puppy. And I absolutely love hearing it – all of it.

They are proud, too, to show me how committed they were to getting a puppy: "Look at all the research we did! Look at how hard we worked! Appreciate just how long we have waited for the right time for our puppy! Trust us, we didn't make this decision on a whim! We want to be good puppy parents!" I nod and agree in all the right places. Yes – you checked every box, you left no form unsubmitted, no question unasked. You honestly did everything I would have recommended, and more.

And after doing all the right things, when their puppy comes home, they tell me stories about the things they did not expect. The things that are going wrong.

> "We don't want the puppy sleeping in our bed, but after four nights of being woken up by him howling in his crate, we can't stand it – we're like zombies. We caved and let him sleep in our bed. How can we get him to sleep in his crate at night?"
>
> "My husband thinks our puppy should do as we tell her, and thinks we're spoiling her by rewarding her with treats. When she doesn't listen to him, he gets really angry and shouts a lot. I don't know what to do, can you help us?"
>
> "We got our puppy from a reputable, licensed breeder, he was in a litter of eight. But since we brought him home, we've noticed he doesn't like other dogs. I'm trying to socialise him and get him used to meeting new dogs. I don't want a nervous puppy. How can I train him to be more confident with other dogs?"
>
> "The kids were playing with the puppy, but yesterday she jumped up and scratched my little girl on the face. Of course I punished the puppy for being aggressive, and I want to book some training to nip this behaviour in the bud, otherwise I'll have to rehome the puppy."

Their frustration and panic starts to creep in because

they've done everything right in advance of bringing their puppy home, and so they weren't expecting things to go wrong. When this happens, it's perfectly normal to panic, to second guess yourself, and even to question if you've made a mistake.

I'd love to say that everyone who goes through this worrying phase immediately looks for professional puppy training and support. But in my experience, there's a period of Googling, trying different things that don't really work, asking friends and family for advice, hoping for an improvement as their puppy grows older, and when none of that stuff works, I usually receive a desperately written, panic fuelled email, pleading for my help with training the puppy.

But not everything can be solved through training. It's important to remember this when you frantically search for puppy trainers in your local area because you're freaking out. Deep down, you're possibly not really ready to commit to training or changing your puppy's behaviour when you're spiralling. You're probably stressing out over what the hell the rest of your life is going to look like with this cute but annoying creature that now lives in your house. You think you want help, but often, you just want someone to tell you your puppy's feral, gremlin-like behaviours, could actually be quite normal.

The same thing happened to me too. In October 2018, adopting my dog, G, wasn't a rushed decision by any means. I had waited 31 years for her. But when she came home, I was completely unprepared for my dream of adopting her to turn into a really difficult, frustrating, worrying and stressful experience. Plus, although I didn't know it at the time, the relationship I was in would crumble a mere few months after bringing G home, which would force me to say goodbye to her.

May 23rd, 2019. Goodbye.

At 7.24 a.m. the urban jungle of South East London, where G and I lived, was already a dangerous animal. Road-rage fuelled drivers raced against the traffic lights, blaring their horns. I remember committing every tiny detail of our goodbye to memory whilst a nauseous pit dug its way into the bottom of my stomach, filling itself with the lingering stench of bin day. Even now, I can still smell London (maybe I need to get that checked out) and feel the dusty gravel of Camberwell Grove clinging to the soles of my trainers, as I resentfully dragged my feet toward the private daycare where I was to leave G for the last time. My ex would collect her later that evening.

I fumbled for the words to let the daycare owner know we were outside. As I waited to hear his familiar, reassuring shuffle down the hallway, I looked down at G to see if she sensed the tsunami of pain ripping through me. I felt like somebody was yanking out my insides and blending them in a grinder. Yet my pain was soon replaced with disappointment, as G, having realised where she was, had eagerly pressed her needle-like snoot against the glossy black paint of the front door, leaving a small souvenir trail of enthusiastic nose drippings. Her tail was wagging with newfound enthusiasm and glee. As far as she was concerned, this was just another day of fun in her new life outside the rescue kennels.

She had no idea that it would only take a couple of steps forward for her to walk completely out of my life. And I didn't have the heart, or the words, to explain this to her. I tried to say goodbye, but I couldn't. It didn't feel real. I pressed the palm of my hand against the heaving pile of bin bags piled up on the communal porch, ready, in the best case, for somebody to pick me up and throw me away. I couldn't understand why, or how, things had gone so horribly wrong with my dog when I had done everything right.

How did we choose G?

I first met G in October 2018, after she had been recommended as a good match for us by the rescue centre. I remember feeling disgusted as I sidestepped the piles of poo she'd dumped around her kennel. My first impressions were pitiful: she was long and skinny, with a disproportionately deep chest – almost as if somebody had blown a balloon into her stomach. Her long, pointy face resembled a knitting needle stuck inside a ball of brindle yarn. She stank to high hell and her breath could have knocked you over. I didn't fall in love with her at first sight – how could I?

But I was desperate for a dog, and any dog would do. So I waited for my emotions to override my disgust, I waited for my excitement to build, happy nerves to kick in, perhaps even tears of relief and joy. Honestly? None of that happened until the day she came home.

I chose G because in my desperate naivety and excitement about bringing a dog home, I made the excellently stupid decision to ignore my gut instinct that she was not the right dog for us. I was doubtful of my ability to care for her, unsure of my feelings towards her, and upset that I did not love her immediately. Of course, my ex had fallen in love with her at first sight, so I clutched onto his positivity and happiness and forced it to be mine. A quiet little voice squeaked in the back of my mind, warning me not to rush into a decision. To think sensibly, rationally, and logically. A louder voice screeched that I was superficial and judgmental, undeserving of the privilege of rescuing a dog from a dirty kennel and terrible life. I allowed myself to be swept up in the emotional riptide of the adoption process, and that's how we chose G as our dog.

They say you don't get a second chance to make a first impression, but that wasn't true for us. My first impression of G was that she was not the dog I wanted, and my second impression was that she desperately needed someone who could see her potential, not just her problems.

Second Chance at First Impressions

One of the questions I ask my clients is: how did you choose your puppy? Not why, but how. How did you know you wanted *your* particular puppy? What made you decide?

I deliberately ask this question, because when they come to me for help, often they've forgotten why they ever thought it would be a good idea to get a puppy in the first place. There is usually some sort of a breakdown in their relationship and they need a gentle, positive reminder, about the puppy they fell in love with.

Over the years, I've heard so many different answers to my question, but there's a few that stand out. I've worked with clients who didn't want the puppy they brought home – no judgement; it happens. Instead, they felt sorry for the puppy, pitied it living on its own whilst its brothers and sisters had found their forever homes, and so they took it home. Others rescued a puppy from a terrible back-yard breeding situation. Nursed the puppy back to health, and fell in love along the way. This is how one particular couple, both in their late seventies, ended up with a husky pup when they really wanted a miniature something-or-other.

Sometimes, for my clients with rescue puppies, a particular photo draws their attention for much longer than the others: a little puppy face they cannot forget. And an adoption profile that reads like an advert:

> "Pippin is a gorgeous and loving boy who hasn't had the best start in life [*I would read this as: Pippin has issues, but it's not his fault*]. He adores human company and will happily sit on your lap all day [*Pippin will probably bark his head off and shit on your carpet if you dare to leave him home alone*].
>
> "This sweet pup can find it difficult to make new dog friends [*he will rip their heads off if you get too close*] which is why he would benefit from further socialisation [*he's currently locked up in a kennel with hundreds of other dogs, but you should definitely force him to meet more dogs*]. We feel Pippin would be best suited to an adult-only home [*we don't want your kids winding him up, and then having him sent back when he retaliates*]."

But let's be honest — you're probably still thinking about the photograph pasted onto the adoption profile rather than the accompanying words. So don't take this the wrong way when I say first impressions don't really matter when you meet your puppy. Probably because puppies are cute and your brain does that thing of "Ooh I want to take them all home with me."

The rational, sensible part of your brain is shoved outside

and silenced, whilst the fun feelings have a brain house party. This is why ethical breeders ask you to visit again and again and again. It's also why reputable rescues ask you to go away and come back when you've really thought things through. The really good rescues will make you jump through burning hoops, test your patience with endless paperwork, lay down the rules, and pounce on you if they get so much as a whiff of hesitation about whether you really are prepared to take on a rescue pup.

The second time you met your puppy probably didn't feel quite the same as the first time. I don't know why this happened to you, but if you want to tell me your story, I would love to hear it. Likewise, if you had a Disney-like expectation of how your life would change when you brought your puppy home, only to find reality didn't match up, you're definitely not alone in feeling this way.

Expectation vs reality: bringing your puppy home

> "We brought him home from the breeder's house, took him in the garden for a wee, sat down in the lounge with him and then stared at each other, wondering what the hell we were supposed to do next."

Nothing can really prepare you for the first few days or weeks of bringing your puppy home. Your whole life is thrown into a topsy-turvy chaos. Of course there is lots of advice about what you should be doing: let puppy out to toilet in the garden, show puppy where they should sleep, crate train them, toilet train them, socialise them, feed them the same food as the breeder for the first few weeks, let them settle in... but honestly, even if you do all those things, it's perfectly natural to make yourself sick with nerves and then do the second worst thing you can do — turn to the Internet for answers to your questions.

In my case, driven by my desperation for a happily ever after ending, and with no resistance from my ex, on October 26th, 2018, we formally adopted G. I remember shifting my bum uncomfortably around on a cheap plastic chair inside one of the consulting rooms at the rescue centre. G was pacing around, sniffing underneath the door. She wouldn't be coming home with us on the same day, as she was due to be spayed later that week. Her coming-home date was eagerly marked in our calendar, along with a massive shopping list of things we thought she needed. A couple of days later, we got a call saying her spay had been brought forward, and she was allowed to come home post-surgery. Instantly, I was plunged way out of my depth, having never cared for a dog, much less a dog sporting wounds across her nether regions.

The first few days of welcoming her home were pretty disgusting. We couldn't bathe her, due to her stitches, so we had to put up with a rancid dog smell in our otherwise lovely home. She didn't appreciate our attempts to toilet train her, and liked to poo in our lounge, and then eat her own turds. We didn't do any training with her because we were so massively overwhelmed by her presence. We had no idea where to start, or what to do.

I had never picked up dog poo before — so living with a poo-eating, stinking dog was definitely somewhat of a shock to my system. Ironically, though, I didn't ask for help straight away. I didn't even know who to ask for help — the rescue centre had seemed a bit too eager to palm her off onto us, so I didn't want to tell them I was struggling. In those early days, it was also difficult to ask for help because I didn't know what was normal and what wasn't.

Help! Help! HELP!

There is a folder in my Inbox labelled Help, where I file emails from prospective clients.

There's one particular email I received whilst a new puppy parent was trying to enjoy a staycation: his puppy was ruining his holiday, and his life. From chewing the furniture, to jumping up at strangers, to whining whenever he left the room — if I was to believe the client, his puppy was the devil incarnate. Over a consultation call the client ranted about the puppy's behaviour, and when I asked how I could help, his answer was not surprising. "Well, I don't know, I've never had a puppy before. I suppose this is what puppies do isn't it. I asked my friend and she told me it took two years for her puppy to start behaving normally."

You see, not everyone who asks for help, actually wants it. And it is a bitter pill to swallow when you run a business based on helping people to raise, train and socialise their puppies. But thinking back to when we had G, I also struggled with asking for help. In fact, when I did ask for help, it actually became part of the problem. The rescue centre offered advice that proved as useless as it was ineffective.

One afternoon I phoned to ask for a solution to stop G from eating her poo. Their advice was to add a tin of pineapple to her food, as this would make her poo taste bad (as if it tasted nice in the first place). What actually happened when we implemented their advice was that G, with the delicacy, care and precision of a neurosurgeon, managed to daintily demolish everything in her food bowl – except for the carefully hidden pieces of pineapple.

I asked for their advice on how to get her used to being left home alone, how to improve her recall, and how to stop her from jumping up at strangers. Each time, I implemented their advice, only to make absolutely no progress with G's training. I was disappointed, disgusted by the feral behaviours of my dream dog, but equally undeterred. I needed things to get better, quickly. So I asked my boss for flexi-leave to help G settle in, and to fast-track her training. I wanted help, but I wasn't ready to accept it from anyone other than myself.

The End

It wasn't the lack of training, socialisation or dog-owning knowledge that forced G and I to part ways. It wasn't her crippling separation anxiety, disgusting poo-eating habits, naughtiness in the park, and penchant for disappearing to chase squirrels that led me to proclaim "enough is enough!" Training G only formed a small, relatively insignificant part of our relationship. Of course, life would have been much easier if she wasn't such a basket case, but when you welcome a dog into your life, you do whatever it takes, for however long you can. It may be easier to believe that G and I parted ways due to the enormity of the training challenges I faced with her, especially considering how inexperienced I was at the time.

However, we said goodbye because of the very real, very painful decay of my human relationshit (not a typo) with my ex. When our relationship had deteriorated to the point of no return, I discovered that he had full legal ownership of her. And there wasn't a damn thing I could do about it. According to UK law, I had no legal rights to G during our breakup. On paper, I did not exist. My name was not registered on her microchip. My signature was not scrawled at the bottom of her adoption paperwork. The dog I had fed, clothed, cared for, and loved harder than I have ever loved anyone before, was not mine to keep.

Our fairytale beginning had soured into a fizzled-out ending. Despite years of patience and preparation, due diligence, dutiful commitment and understanding of the responsibility of getting a dog, the moral of this particular story is that you really can do everything right, only for everything to go wrong.

In all honesty, and in search of a silver lining, G is the reason why I founded Meera Puppins. Without the chaos and havoc she brought into my life, I would never have understood or experienced the importance, or the impact, of relationships in caring for a dog. You see, caring for your puppy is not easy, as we are led to believe. But it is far too easy to get things wrong. To beat ourselves up for not knowing more or knowing better. For trusting professionals who don't have our puppy's best interests at heart. To believe that everyone else has a practically perfect puppy, so it must be us who are doing things wrong.

G is the reason why I developed a signature puppy training system that is different from everyone else's — it's as simple as it is effective: relationship first, training second. You see, I loved G for who she was, not how she behaved. I'd like you to think about this if you're struggling like I was. Training is not the be all and end all, not everything can be resolved through more training, as I've just proved by sharing my dog-owning-failure story with you.

In fact, training your puppy is possibly one of the hardest things that you can do. This brings me to Lie Number 2 – that puppy training is easy, and you're probably just doing it wrong.

Practically Perfect Puppy Lie Number 2

Puppy training is easy, you're probably doing it wrong

Puppy training is not easy.

"Training our puppy is much harder than I thought it would be."

"We must be doing something wrong; this isn't what we wanted to happen."

"We went to puppy classes, but they don't work outside when it's just me and the puppy."

"I don't know who needs the training – the puppy or me!"

"We've been trying to train him ourselves, but things are getting worse."

"She's three now, and she still has the same naughty habits as when she was a puppy."

These are all things that puppy owners and clients have shared with me. To read them, and then say that puppy training is easy, is a lie. And yes, there probably are some things that you're doing wrong. But how can I expect you to get it right when you're not a professional puppy trainer?

Having trained and socialised hundreds of lovely puppies, it's my experience that you might find training your puppy difficult because you're expecting too much too quickly. Often I'll hear things like, "It's been a week and he still isn't sleeping through the night," or "We brought her home two days ago and it's been a nightmare!"

Naturally, when you're sleep deprived, everything seems to take much longer. And then you might feel frustrated because you aren't making the progress that you want to, as quickly as you want to. I've also worked with clients who have looked for professional puppy support from other trainers, and then confided that they felt bombarded, overwhelmed, or disappointed, rather than supported.

Truth is, the puppy training industry isn't regulated, which means anyone and everyone can call themselves a trainer – which doesn't really help you, if you don't know which trainer red flags to watch out for.

Navigating the minefield of puppy training

Puppy training isn't easy because nobody can really agree on anything, and every trainer you go to will have a different way of training.

When I had G, I was starting to resent being a dog mum, which is when I started to be more proactive about training her myself. I began to devour dog training information like I do my favourite crisps – by the bagful. I crunched my way through packets of dog training reports, tore into shiny dog magazines, and ripped into multiple social media accounts led by famous dog trainers. But I only liked a few of the flavours of the advice I was chewing my way through.

Some trainers advocated for punishment, harsh methods and techniques that made me feel queasy. Other trainers berated the choices of these aversive trainers, yet they didn't offer any real advice on how to resolve the behavioural issues we were experiencing. The whole thing felt utterly hopeless and pointless.

G had extreme separation anxiety — we literally couldn't leave her for a second. I remember having a consultation call with a trainer who specialised in separation anxiety, to the tune of £1,500 and with no guarantee that the training would help us. At the time, I was horrified — how could I justify paying that much money with no guarantee the training would even work? Now, as a trainer myself, I understand much more about the complexities and nuances of behavioural training and rehabilitation — and the price tag that comes with that knowledge.

If you think about training your puppy as consistently teaching them new habits, until the new habits become the norm, it's easier to appreciate why training can be so difficult. Maybe you've experienced this yourself: perhaps you've tried to stick to a diet, or to quit smoking. It's not easy is it? It takes a lot of effort, willpower and motivation to repeat the same things over and over again, until you finally get to where you want to be. Puppy training is a little bit like this too: you have to make lots of changes to push past the icky bits, and it is anything but easy.

But why is it so hard to train my puppy?

There are a few reasons why it's so difficult to train your puppy:

1. You make things much harder than they need to be.
2. Everyone has an opinion on the "right" way to train your puppy, and hardly anyone agrees with each other.
3. You might meet three types of puppy trainers along your puppy training journey, two of whom will not help you.
4. You've focused so hard on training your puppy to be perfect that you've forgotten about your relationship with your puppy, which can cause a communication breakdown, and means you're easily frustrated and annoyed, and your puppy is confused about what you want them to do.

Of course there are many more reasons why training your puppy might be difficult.

For example, if they're on crate rest due to illness or injury, they might be bored and less likely to listen to you. Or you might be trying to train them in an environment that's too distracting or exciting — imagine someone asking you to solve algebra equations whilst you're enjoying a luxury beach holiday; you're probably not going to get very far, are you?

When I work with my private puppy clients, I host the sessions at their homes, and in their local areas. These are environments where the puppy feels safe, comfortable and confident, which usually means they pick the training up much faster. But puppy training doesn't always have to take place at your home. I teach my group puppy classes in a fabulous café, because I know how puppies learn, how to motivate them, and how to support you along the way.

The problem with puppy trainers: the good, the terrible, and the dangerous

The puppy training industry is not regulated, which means anyone can call themselves a puppy trainer. This makes it really difficult for you to spot the difference between the good trainers, the terrible ones and the downright dangerous ones. Something else that no-one will tell you is there's a lot of in-fighting between trainers – on everything from which treats to use, to which words to say. Is it a cue or is it a command? I say, does it actually matter?

With the caveat that if your trainer hits, punishes or shouts at your puppy, or if they rely on inflicting pain as a training tool, then buyer beware, grab your pup and run for the hills.

If you work with me, we'll follow my signature puppy training system, which is based on prioritising your relationship with your puppy, then following kind, gentle and reward-based training techniques. But a different trainer might tell you this namby-pamby approach will ruin your puppy and turn them into a hapless adult dog. So if you are feeling confused, fed up or frustrated when it comes to training, raising and socialising your puppy, the good news is that you're not alone – and hopefully you're starting to understand why it really is a minefield!

A good trainer will help you without hurting your

puppy. Yes, it is almost as simple as that. We will often ask you lots of questions and get to know you; sometimes, we will want to work alongside your vet to make sure your puppy isn't experiencing any niggling pain or discomfort that could be making things worse.

Sometimes behaviours get worse before they get better, and often progress is slow and steady because the process of training and changing behaviour isn't a quick-fix. It's not a sexy way of working, but it is honest, transparent and ethical. At each stage of the journey, we will have your puppy's best interests at heart. We will take our time and work with you, using positive and reward-based training techniques.

We don't wave a magic wand and abracadabra your puppy's problems away. Whilst we are willing to work with you and help you, we hope you will trust us and work alongside us, instead of fighting us when you have to put the work in yourself.

But how do I train my puppy?

This is the question I'm asked most frequently — but as I told you earlier, this isn't a technical puppy training book. The question you should be asking, although no one ever does, is actually, "How does my puppy learn?"

Most puppy owners throw their puppies into the deep end of the training pool whether they have the skills to swim or not. I'm going to let you in on a little secret that will make training your puppy easier: puppies learn all the time — not just when you're training them. Puppies learn through association; they do what works well for them by observing what is happening around them, and how you react to what they're doing.

Your puppy jumps up because this usually gets your attention — good or bad.

Your puppy bites because their teeth are sore, and it feels good to sink them into your flesh or sofa cushions. I've witnessed teething puppies trying to chew their exasperated owner's walls, and I've even witnessed a puppy chewing patio paving slabs. Do these things taste good to your puppy? Probably not, but the relief they experience outweighs the awful taste.

Your puppy's behaviour is a direct form of communication with you. They cry because you've done something to upset them — locking them in their crate, or shutting the bathroom door so you can have a wee in peace. All day long, your puppy learns what they like and what they don't. They might like it when you put your shoes on and grab their lead because this means they're going out. Equally, they may howl, jump up or bite you if you put your shoes on and then crate them — because this means they will be left home alone.

Puppies are much more intelligent than most people give them credit for. Quicker than you can say "treat" they will learn which behaviours you like and which behaviours make you shout. Puppies learn a lot without any training at all. One of my client's puppies will beg for a treat whenever her mum or siblings are in the kitchen, but she doesn't try it on when her dad is in the kitchen. Why? Because she knows her dad won't give in and fetch her a treat from the jar. She wasn't trained to do this — she learnt from observing her owners' reactions to her behaviours. Clever, huh?

The sticky point comes when your puppy does things you don't like, and you need to teach them what you want them to do instead. This is often when unhelpful labels come into practice: my puppy is being stubborn, my puppy is being naughty, my puppy did a revenge poo because I left him home alone for an hour (I wish I was kidding, but someone actually said this to me!) Sorry but this simply isn't true, nor is it helpful. Now I've explained how your puppy learns, are things starting to make more sense?

If you want to train your puppy to either start doing things i.e. sleeping in their own bed, or stop doing things i.e. stop barking at the postman, there's a few things you need to think about:

- What is your puppy's motivation? Why should they *want* to do the thing you want them to do?
- How are you going to teach your puppy there's a better alternative to stop them doing the thing they really like?
- Are you making proactive changes to your puppy's environment to help them be more successful in their training, or are you half-assing things?

As this isn't a technical puppy training book, I don't want to bombard you with more stuff. But I will say that if you'd like to have a chat about something specific, you can book a complimentary call with me via my website.

I'd also like to point out that your puppy's personality and their behaviour are not the same thing – your puppy may be a cuddle bug at home, the sweetest, snooziest, loveliest pup to have ever existed, and then transform into a raging, barking, reactive, gobshite on a lead when you're out on your walks. Their personality has not changed, but their behaviour has. This is a really important, yet often overlooked distinction to make.

Personality vs. Behaviour

We change our behaviour all the time. We behave differently when we're bored or stressed out at work, compared to when we're out socialising with friends. We may be on our best behaviour when spending time with our partner's family, and then act like utter slobs when we're back in our own homes. Our behaviour changes to match our environment and it's the same with puppies — except we usually don't see it that way.

Your training may work in the lounge, but not in the garden, or in the park. This is because the environment has changed to a more exciting, fun or distracting one. If you're struggling with this, a decent trainer will be able to pick out exactly what the problem is, and help you get over this hurdle. Don't despair, it is absolutely possible!

Remember, your puppy's personality and their behaviour are not the same thing! One of the things I hear most often is, "She's a lovely puppy at home, but behaves hideously when we're outside," or "He's such a sweet, happy, loving puppy, but I dread taking him for walks, it's so embarrassing when he jerks me around on the lead!" These are examples of not separating your puppy's personality and their behaviour, and then falling into the trap of thinking that everything your puppy is doing needs to be resolved through training. Training, training and more training.

Often I'm asked to help shy or nervous puppies become more sociable, through "getting them used to meeting other dogs." In fact, there's lots of things puppy owners want their pooches to get used to: noisy traffic, bigger or smaller dogs, being left home alone, busy parks, their crate, going for walks in the rain, or in the dark — the list is endless! Each time there seems to be a thought process that runs along the lines of, "Hmmm, my puppy is scared of this thing. I know what I'll do, I'll make them spend loads of time around the scary thing, and that will help them get used to it."

Sounds ridiculous doesn't it? Let me ask you what you are scared of. And how would you feel if I trapped you into doing the scary thing every day? Would you get over your fear and get used to it, or would you absolutely hate what I was doing to you and then start to behave really erratically, to try and avoid the scary thing? Thought so!

Don't make the mistake of believing your puppy needs to "get used to" scary things. Instead, try and tell yourself that your puppy may need your help in not being scared of the scary thing. Do the equivalent of checking under their bed for monsters, and don't belittle them for having big feelings about little things.

Training is not always the answer to every single thing you don't like about your puppy. Especially if some of their cheeky behaviours are part of their personality. In that case, you want to think more about managing and controlling the environment. I'd really recommend spending a little time thinking about this, and separate your puppy's behaviour from their personality — especially if you're looking to sign up for puppy training, because training and behaviour are also not the same thing.

I wish I had met you sooner

As I talked about earlier, there are good, bad and downright dangerous trainers — and sadly, I've had a few clients come to me after having horrible experiences with other trainers. Each time, they've said, "I wish I had met you sooner" because of the massive sense of relief they feel when they're talking to me.

I take my time to listen, understand the problems you're having, and then work with you to find appropriate solutions. Sometimes that means working with you on a 1:1 basis, and other times that means referring you to a fellow professional if you're coming to me with a training problem I can't comfortably help you to resolve.

When choosing your puppy trainer, don't ignore your gut instinct. If something feels wrong or makes you feel a bit icky, then something probably is wrong.

Bobby's Story

Unfortunately, not every puppy training story has a happily ever after ending, and sometimes trainers can make things worse, not better. Bobby's story happens more than you might think, and I wanted to share it because I want you to see how easy it is to get sucked into the promises of a downright dangerous trainer.

As a puppy, Bobby's owners noticed that he was pulling on his lead quite a bit, which is a really common behaviour that can be improved with consistent training. Now, whilst the old adage of "size doesn't matter" may not apply in real life, it does when it comes to puppy training. Call it double standards, but the bigger the puppy, the more pressure there is to train perfect behaviours. There is less tolerance when a 30kg puppy jumps up at a stranger, compared to a miniature poodle doing the same thing.

We are quick to label big dogs as dangerous, out of control or aggressive. For small dogs, we laugh, make stupid comments like, "Oh does he think he's a big dog" and we're much more tolerant of the same behaviours we would never accept in big dogs.

As you can probably guess, Bobby was a big puppy and as an adult, his parents knew he could easily weigh over 40kg, so it's not hard to understand why they wanted to nip the lead pulling in the bud. Feeling like it wasn't something they could tackle on their own, they looked for professional help and enrolled Bobby into a group puppy class — so far, so great, right? When you're stuck, frustrated, or unsure of what you're doing, it's the most normal thing to look for someone to help you.

Bobby's group-class trainer liked to spend the first ten minutes of each session talking to the owners. Now, if you've ever stopped to briefly chat to someone whilst out with your puppy, you'll know that a) your puppy has a short attention span, and b) they will get bored really quickly if you don't give them something to do, and they will probably start dicking around.

This is what happened in Bobby's class. So the trainer encouraged the owners to throw handfuls of food onto the ground, to give the pups something to do. But Bobby, and a few of the other pups, soon tired of that activity — especially when there were other fun puppies to play with! So when the trainer let the pups off the lead, they were so excited they would run around, play and do their own thing.

Instead of making progress in the group training classes,

Bobby was whirling around in circles. Pointless, unhelpful circles. At this stage, it's easy to understand how frustration can set in: here you are, doing all the right things, looking for help, and yet you're not making any progress.

After finishing the classes, but no closer to solving the problem they had in the first place, Bobby's owners decided to take matters into their own hands and have a go at training him themselves. But there was a problem. Bobby wasn't responding to training with treats.

A note on training your puppy with treats

When Bobby's mum reached out to me for 1:1 help, I explained that I use treats as part of my training sessions. And yes, I panicked a bit when she said that Bobby didn't respond to treat-based training. Why? Because when you work with me I often use food as part of my training plans. But shovelling treats at your puppy isn't actually training them. Throwing handfuls of food onto the ground for your puppy isn't always going to help your puppy feel better about what's happening around them. Treats are not the answer to everything!

A trainer who is worth the treats in their pocket will know how to use food to *support* their teaching and training, not to replace it. We will also think about things you probably won't – such as distance, duration and difficulty. If your puppy is too stressed out to take treats, the problem is usually not the treats. If a puppy is too close to the scary thing, if they're tired or bored of the training, or if what you're asking them to do is too difficult, then yes, your puppy probably isn't going to be that interested in taking treats from you. Think about it, if you found yourself walking down a dark street, alone at night, terrified that something bad would happen to you, would it help you feel safer if someone was trying to spoon food into your mouth? Or would your priority be to get the hell out of dodge?

I've lost count of the amount of times I've seen puppy owners trying to force treats into their puppy's mouths, with the treats disappearing into puppy's eyes, ears and nose, whilst the puppy's body language is screaming "get me out of here!" Inevitably, the treats get the blame.

Whilst you digest all that (pun intended), I want to share what Bobby's mum wrote to me when I asked for her permission to share Bobby's story. She said: "You showed us how to reward him with different kinds of treats (to be fair, the first guy did this), but he just liked the sound of his voice and would talk about nothing for around 10 mins of our 30 min lesson! You are kind, gentle and very knowledgeable."

And there you have it. It's not the treats that make a difference; it's finding a trainer who knows how to use them. I'm lucky to see Bobby on a regular basis, as he comes along to my monthly Teenage Training Treks. At the last trek, Bobby's mum joked with me that he only misbehaves because he wants to spend more time with me.

What did Bobby do next?

Before my slight digression on treats, I told you how Bobby wasn't responding to treats as part of his DIY training. This prompted his parents to look for a trainer that was not treat-based. They had already tried traditional group classes, tried training Bobby themselves, and it's easy to empathise with the frustration that can build up. Bobby's parents stumbled upon a trainer who promised great things, and delivered nothing but awful advice and heavy-handed training techniques. The initial issues of Bobby pulling on his lead, and sometimes pulling his owners in the direction of other dogs, hadn't been fully resolved.

In Bobby's first lesson, the new trainer swapped Bobby's normal lead for a rope lead, which he slung over Bobby's head and tightened around his neck. Whenever Bobby pulled forward, the rope would tighten around his neck, which was painful. Bobby soon realised if he pulled, he would feel pain. So he stopped pulling and boom, problem solved!

Or so you might think. The problem with using pain as a training tool (aside from the ethics) is that over time, most dogs will accept the pain and revert back to the behaviours you're trying to stop. This means, over time, you'll find your trainer encouraging you to increase the amount of pain you're inflicting, which is just vile.

This particular trainer decided that choking Bobby wasn't enough pain, he also wanted to control Bobby's interactions with other dogs. As Bobby was a friendly and sociable puppy, he would sometimes pull his parents in the direction of other dogs. The trainer's advice was to keep Bobby away from other dogs at all times, and not to let him off his lead. Now you might shoot me, but I agree that prevention and management of unwanted behaviours are a core part of training — but only when handled responsibly and ethically. What the trainer was asking for was extreme: a complete ban on seeing other dogs during his socialisation stage. Can you guess what kind of impact this had on Bobby?

Training session number two was a recap of pain and punishment.

Session three was another reason you should be highly

choosy before picking a trainer. In lesson 3, Bobby learned that the sight of another dog would also result in a punishment for him. The trainer pulled a dog out of his trailer and paraded him around for Bobby to see. Naturally, Bobby was curious to check out his new playmate and pulled over to say hi. At this point, the trainer yanked Bobby so hard by the rope around his neck, that he lifted him clean off the ground and into the air.

What do you think the trainer was trying to teach Bobby? The second time around, it was Bobby's turn to be paraded in front of the stooge dog, and Bobby was so afraid of what would happen next, that he cowered down onto the ground instead of pulling to say hello.

Do you think that means the trainer did a good job? My opinion is too explicitly expletive to be printed.

I've shared Bobby's story because training isn't easy. Finding a decent puppy trainer is definitely not easy. It's not easy for you, it's rarely easy for your puppy, and it's not easy for me to pick up the pieces when your puppy has been hurt in the name of training.

After this horrible experience, you can imagine how upset Bobby's parents were feeling. They felt like they'd tried lots of things, and wisely decided to kick that trainer to the kerb. Bobby's behaviours had gotten much worse — almost like a reverse effect from the training. Whereas previously they had been able to manage the pulling, it was now out of control. After being banned from meeting other dogs, Bobby literally couldn't contain his excitement when he saw them. He couldn't focus on anything other than meeting the other dogs. Whatever the trainer had done to Bobby, it definitely didn't improve matters.

Why find someone else?

You might think that after trying two different trainers, but still experiencing problems, Bobby's parents were just throwing good money after bad by getting in touch with me. Perhaps you're thinking you wouldn't have bothered to find someone else, or you would have just taken a break from training altogether.

With Bobby, we worked together over the course of several 1:1 sessions and it was clear that Bobby was really confused about what was expected of him, which is hardly surprising!

In our first session, Bobby tried to climb and hump me. His mum was mortified, as Bobby was almost taller than me when standing on his back legs, but I realised he was probably feeling overexcited and overwhelmed. We did make some progress during our training sessions, working mainly on teaching Bobby to walk nicely on his lead (a normal lead, not a choke lead!) and to come back to us from seeing other dogs. But Bobby's training is still ongoing, because a lot of damage had been done, and it takes a long time for young dogs to normalise new, positive experiences.

Bobby is still making slow but steady progress, and enjoys being treated for his good behaviour. I absolutely love him to pieces, he's playful and goofy and has the most gorgeous personality. I love the relationship I have with Bobby, and his mum tells me that he's always checking for me when we're out on our treks and I'm not in Bobby's line of sight. This isn't something you can achieve only with training; your puppy needs to trust you, and to believe that you really do have their back – which is part of my signature puppy training system.

MeeraPuppins signature puppy training system: relationships first, training second

At Meera Puppins, I have a signature puppy training system that starts with relationships, and is different from what everyone else tells you to do with your puppy. Now don't get me wrong, it is essential to toilet train your puppy, so you don't have to rip up all your carpets. It's crucial to teach them good bite inhibition, so you don't end up in jail over a dog bite. And you must gently encourage them to be independent so you can enjoy your lives together and apart. Now, whilst all those things *are* essential, they are not the *most* important when you first get your puppy.

My style of puppy training is based on the belief that if you can help your puppy feel safe, confident and comfortable in your company, then training your puppy will be much easier. We never start any human relationships with training — could you imagine how that would go down?

> "Sorry, Steve, but until you have been trained to chew with your mouth shut, you are banned from eating in the staff cafeteria."
>
> "On our first date I was asked to sit and wait before I could eat my meal. Every time I reached to take a mouthful, I had to sit, perform a trick, and only then was I allowed to eat."
>
> "When walking with my friend, if I stepped ahead of her, I received a slap to the back of my head, to teach me to walk next to her."

It's funny, but also quite sad. We expect so much from our puppies, and often we mistakenly buy into the "nothing in life is for free" style of training — which means that every time our puppy wants something, we make them perform first. Puppy is only allowed a treat if they sit and do paw. Puppy is only allowed on the sofa if they sit and beg. Puppy must walk next to us at all times on their walks if they want to enjoy off-lead privileges. Puppy must sit and wait for their food. Puppy must never pull on their lead.

Why? Do you sit and wait for your food at every meal? Every time you enjoy a treat, do you run a lap round the garden first? Honestly — please enlighten me as to why we do these things to our puppies. What is the point of doing these things to them?

In order to break this cycle, can I ask you to think about why you got a puppy in the first place — and the warm, cute, fuzzy feeling that came along with them. Can you still remember your Disney-like dream of frolicking for hours together in the countryside, with endless loyalty and companionship, unconditional love... and finally having someone to blame your farts on?

Why did you forget these things when you brought your puppy home? What's happened to make you second guess everything you're doing? Why do you think a random stranger on the internet (I'm referring to the terrible and dangerous trainers here) knows your puppy better than you do? At best, you will terrify your puppy. At worst, you will ruin your relationship with your pup. Yes — your relationship. Puppy ownership is a two-way street; you can't blindly bulldoze your way down it and not expect to crash along the way.

Relationshits vs relationships

Let's be honest; no matter what I say about training your puppy, sometimes your puppy will just be downright annoying. And yes, it's okay to feel slightly resentful of the things you gave up for them. This is what I refer to as a relationshit. Relationshits are the struggles of raising the puppy you wanted whilst not understanding the puppy you have. Relationshits is the term I'm going to use to describe all the shitty parts of your relationship with your puppy.

Raising a puppy is as frustrating as it is difficult. That doesn't mean that you don't love them or that they aren't good boys or girls. It just means you're experiencing what most puppy owners are too embarrassed or ashamed to talk about. So let's talk about it now, in Lie Number 3 — that relationshits (not a typo) aren't real.

Practically Perfect Puppy Lie Number 3

Relationshits (not a typo) aren't real

R*elationshits* – as much as my editing software insists on telling me otherwise, this is not a typo. *Relationshit* refers to all the shitty parts of your relationship with your puppy and the knock-on stressful effect it can also cause in your human relationships.

This is probably the first time you're reading about relationshits in a book about puppies. Congratulations, what you're about to read will be as enlightening as it is reassuring. You are not alone; this is a safe space. It's ok to admit that getting your puppy was lovely, but also bloody hard work, frustrating to the point of exhaustion, and physically painful – why are puppy teeth so sharp?! Let's not forget how much fun it was to raise your puppy on a nightly average of about two hours sleep.

Think about it for a second. You've welcomed an entirely different species into your home, and neither of you speak the same language or share the same interests (unless you're into cocking your leg against lampposts and eating soil). You work hard to put food in your puppy's bowl, to keep your home clean, warm and safe. Whereas your puppy lives rent-free, doesn't pay any bills, doesn't have a job, and generates regular expenses. Your puppy lounges around all day, sleeping on the sofa you swore they wouldn't be allowed on, gets under your feet and stealthily lies in your doorways, with the sole aim of tripping you up. Neither of you understands the other's purpose in life.

Your puppy wonders: why are you always rushing? Why do you always look so stressed? Why don't you nap during the day?

And you wonder... why do you have to sniff EVERYTHING?! Including people's crotches. Why do you lie down in the middle of a walk and refuse to move?! Why do you whine whenever I leave the room? Why do you repeatedly try to kill yourself by eating stones from the garden and rubbish off the street? Do you secretly HATE ME?!

One of the biggest reasons why you might end up in a relationshit with your puppy, is because you both expect ridiculous things from each other, and have no idea how to achieve them.

What is a relationshit?

A relationshit is a reference to the pain you've felt (or are feeling) at raising your puppy. Puppies are fluffy, cute, tiny, and gorgeous; maybe that's why we put up with their shit. Puppies are fuzzy little gremlins. Sometimes they are annoying; quite often, they are demanding. They will eat up every minute of your day, chew on the last few threads of your sanity, dabble in deathly adventures and make you question why you have decided to torture yourself in this way. They will repay your efforts to train, socialise and exercise them by either gassing you out with their farts (for tiny bums they do produce the most ungodly smells), chewing your house to shreds, and using your limbs as moving targets for their biting. If you're nodding along and thinking, "Omg, yes! Finally! Someone telling the truth about puppy ownership!" then let me reassure you that you are not alone.

I particularly like the way Urban Dictionary has three separate definitions for relationshits. They're talking about human relationshits, but this is a book about puppies, so I've interpreted their definitions accordingly.

a) "One person in the relationship doesn't want to be there."

In my experience, this is usually the stressed-out puppy owner, who was desperate to get a puppy, but was nowhere near prepared for the reality of bringing their pup home. The stressed-out puppy owner lies awake at night, tortured by the cries of their puppy locked up in a crate downstairs. The stressed-out puppy owner believes they must "start as they mean to go on", even if it means walking around in a zombie state due to sleep deprivation. The stressed-out puppy owner has been told not to comfort their crying puppy, despite every moral fibre urging them to go downstairs and help their scared, lonely puppy. After a few nights of military-style sleep deprivation torture, the stressed-out puppy owner decides to sleep downstairs on the sofa and then makes thinly veiled jokes about how their puppy is ruling the roost — and their lives.

What a horrible relationshit to be in. Not understanding your puppy's basic needs for companionship and comfort is distressing to you and your puppy. By allowing your puppy to sleep near you, especially during the first few weeks of bringing them home, you are teaching your puppy that they are safe, they are home, and that you've got their back. For god's sake, forget what the training books say, and stop Googling. Right now, take every idea/theory/opinion you have on "puppy dominance" and set it on fire. Prioritise building a safe, positive and happy relationship with your puppy — which starts with a good night's sleep for both of you. Trust me, you'll both be happier!

b) "Both people in the relationship don't want to be there."

Unless you've rescued your puppy from a horrible situation, generally speaking, your puppy was probably having a great time with his/her parents and littermates. Then you came along, and everything about your puppy's life changed. Perhaps you haven't thought about it that way, but that's why I wrote this book. To make you rethink and improve your relationship with your puppy.

One of the main causes of frustration is often a lack of understanding of what each party needs, and how to fulfil those needs. You need your puppy to be trained up quickly so you can enjoy your life and not feel like a prisoner in your own home. You need to go to work, to leave your puppy home alone and to go out and see your friends and family. You need your puppy to be trusted not to eat your house when you are gone. You need a break away from your puppy sometimes. I totally get it — one of my friends actually says that if everyone had a puppy before they had kids, people would stop having kids. Puppies are a massive, time-consuming commitment.

But what does your puppy need from you? Your puppy has a simple set of needs: to feel safe, comfortable, loved, healthy and happy. In themselves, these are not difficult needs. Until you add a human who doesn't know how to provide these things.

Puppies have the attention span of toddlers fed a diet of ice cream and sweets — approximately 0.02 seconds if you're lucky. This is another massive cause of frustration, especially when you expect your puppy to perform perfect behaviours from day one. Instead of blindly following what everyone else is doing, think about the things that are important to you, and what's important to your puppy. Can you meet each other in the middle? Sometimes less training and more relationship building is what's actually needed.

c) *One or both of the relationshit-ers want to decapitate the other member of the relationship.*

This is usually accurate for couples who have chosen to welcome a puppy. It's rare for both partners to fully agree on how to train, raise and care for the puppy. Eventually, when things are at breaking point, there is a decision to call in a professional puppy trainer or enrol the puppy into classes because the couple wants an impartial third party to tell them what to do, so they stop fighting with each other. Chewing, biting, weeing on everything in sight, jumping and gnawing the house apart is normal puppy behaviour. And whilst it is entirely normal, it is also very problematic because it is annoying as hell.

Puppy house of horrors

It's often so easy to underestimate the strain of a new puppy on your human relationships. I remember taking on a new puppy client who had come to me for help with toilet training her puppy, establishing a peaceful sleeping routine, and working through the pup's separation anxiety. She got in touch not just to resolve the behaviours but because the puppy was putting a huge and heavy strain on her relationship with her partner. Whilst her approach to training their puppy was softly-softly, very much aligned with mine, her partner's approach was much more heavy-handed. Between them, they were only confusing the puppy and stirring up tension in their household until it was hanging in the air like a great big thick custardy goop that threatened to plop down from the ceiling and drown them in its gunky gunge.

Whilst I empathised with their situation, I didn't realise the depth of the conflict or the extent of the impact it was having on the puppy until I turned up on their doorstep, naively eager for our first training session. Armed with papers, case studies, a training plan and a notebook full of prompts, I was unprepared for the house's ice-cold, frigid atmosphere. A creepy sense of terror started to crawl along my spine, inching its way up my neck, curling into my hair and twisting my puppy training senses into a sweaty panic. It was clear that my presence was unwelcome by the puppy's dad. As I crossed the threshold into the lounge, I observed the puppy's natural reactions to a visitor in their home and noted the annoyance of puppy's dad. I felt pretty strange, as the house appeared to be warning me...

"You're out of your depth..." the curtains rustled.

"He'll never let you change his heavy-handed tune on how to train the puppy..." gloated the TV remote.

"Hey you, you better stop the bloody puppy from pissing on my legs..." swore the dining room table.

"Hello," said the lady. "My husband's home early from

work so he could join us for the training. I do hope you can help us."

That was one of the most challenging puppy training sessions I've ever had — not because of the puppy but because of his impact on the owners' relationship. Couples, in particular, often think they're looking for a puppy trainer when they're really looking for a neutral third party to tell them what to do, and to be pointed in the direction of an emergency exit. This is so when they're in the throes of a puppy-related argument, instead of pointing fingers at each other and bickering, they can now shift the weight of their puppy-induced stress onto the person they're paying for help.

In this case, the male owner was dead set against every single one of my suggestions and recommendations that I KNEW would help resolve the behavioural issues they were experiencing with their puppy. This made it incredibly difficult to achieve what I had been booked for. I later realised you can't help someone who doesn't want to be helped, especially if they believe they're right about everything. The female owner was much happier to take my suggestions on board and convinced her partner to let her try. I saw them a little while ago, and whilst the human relationship is none of my business, the puppy is thriving, happy and well.

From Shit to Ship

In the Autumn of 2022, I received a phone call from a new puppy mum enquiring about my Practically Perfect Puppy (not a lie) bespoke puppy training package. We ran through the usual questions: what was involved, how much it cost etc.

and what were the benefits of privately training the puppy with me instead of in a group class.

Puppy's mum confessed that they already had a young daughter, and her husband didn't want a puppy, so now she had to prove to him, through training, that this was a great idea and their puppy would be an excellent addition to their family.

"Challenge accepted!" I thought to myself, promising to deliver the best of my puppy training magic, as I wanted the family to enjoy their puppy, whom they named Teddy because he looked like a gorgeous teddy bear.

In our first session, I noticed that Teddy's dad wasn't loving having him home – and I'm not surprised. The breeder advised them to leave him locked in his crate at night, isolated away from his new family, and ignore his constant cries for help. To start with, everyone in the household was sleep deprived. Like most puppies, Teddy was also quite bitey and liked to jump up a lot – not ideal when you have a toddler, and this was just another black mark against the puppy's arrival. Not a great start to getting a puppy that you didn't really want in the first place.

Teddy's dad was already frustrated, and I knew there wasn't much benefit to kicking things off with hardcore training. Instead, I set out to positively transform the relationship between Teddy and his dad, teaching Teddy how to behave in a way his dad liked and showing dad how to understand what Teddy needed – whether it was a wee, a nap, something to chew, or a good old cuddle. To his credit, Teddy's dad took everything I advised on board and started implementing it immediately. This is because the training techniques I showed him really do work when you are shown what to do, and how to do it effectively.

By the end of our five-week training, I had the privilege of witnessing the most incredible transformation of the relationship between Teddy and his dad. Imagine the scene: we're training outside and everything's going really well, when a dog suddenly starts barking really close to Teddy. Teddy's dad has hold of his lead, and noticing that Ted is terrified, his new found dog-dad instincts kick in. He quickly gets down to Teddy's level, scoops him up in his arms and whisks him away from the scary thing. Not wanting Teddy to be scared, he carries him all the way home.

Now, this may not seem like much to you, but bearing in mind that Teddy was a puppy he didn't want, an idea he resisted, an arrival he was hesitant to welcome, the transformation was nothing less than amazing. Having recently caught up with Teddy's family, I'm told that Teddy enjoys napping on his dad's side of the bed, lots of cuddles and a beautiful relationship with his family. We didn't push Teddy into robotic, monotonous training drills and exercises. We worked together based on a kind and gentle understanding of Teddy's needs, and on the importance of relationships when training, raising and caring for your puppy.

Whilst I agree that training can play a huge part in caring for your puppy, I will still argue that relationships should come first, and training should come second. That is not to say you shouldn't train your puppy — don't twist my words. I really do believe that by prioritising a safe and fun relationship with your puppy, the training part will come much easier! This is really important because when puppies are in their ouchy, bitey, fighty stage, lots of puppy owners think they will simply grow out of these behaviours. They excuse their pup's behaviour by saying things like,

"Ah he's only young, he'll learn," or "I'm sure he'll grow out of it."

Well, I hate to be the bearer of bad news, but this is very rarely true — as you'll discover in Lie Number 4: that your puppy will grow out of the behaviours you don't like.

Practically Perfect Puppy Lie Number 4

Your puppy will grow out of it

"I wish I had known that cute behaviours in a 3kg puppy are not cute in a 17kg dog!" This is what Ashley, mum to senior dog Morrie (short for Moriarty, which is an epic name) answered when I asked what she wished she'd known about getting a puppy. Morrie, now nine years old, never grew out of his naughty but cute puppy habits.

I wish I could tell you that puppies grow out of jumping up, chewing or biting. But I'd be lying to you, and that hardly seems fair, seeing as you've made it all the way through to the final chapter of this book.

Puppies, contrary to popular belief, don't grow out of behaviours. What happens instead is, over time, puppy behaviour turns into a habit. By the time they hit their teenage stage (which comes with a natural regression in their training, as their hormones kick in) you'll likely be tearing your hair out, wondering why things aren't getting better now your puppy is older.

Maybe you can relate; perhaps you also believed your puppy would grow out of their "naughty" behaviours, only for the exact opposite to happen. Playful puppy biting or rough-and-tumble play might be cute when dealing with a 4kg bundle of fluff. You might think it's funny when your puppy drags your shoes to their bed and chews up the laces. You may even be flattered when your puppy excitedly jumps up at you. How could you not find these behaviours cute?

But once your puppy is fully grown and weighs the same as a brick powerhouse (assuming you don't have a toy or teacup breed of dog, who will retain their tiny stature well into adulthood) will you still find these behaviours cute or endearing?

But my puppy is so cute when...

I believe we only put up with puppies because they are cute. Seriously — hear me out. If you welcomed a house guest who used your home as an indoor toilet, kept you up all night, chewed your furniture, cried whenever you went out of sight, ate your food and never helped with the housework, you'd soon get fed up. Yet this is precisely what our puppies do and we put up with all of it and more! It's tough to remember that your teeny tiny cutesy wutesy puppy will turn into a big, strong adult. This doesn't make you a bad puppy owner; it just makes you human.

I previously worked with a gorgeous puppy who would bark excessively whenever anyone visited his home. It was a loud, shrill, piercing and stressful bark that would continue well past the visitor walking in and making themselves comfortable. Despite knowing this, when I first walked into my client's home for our private training sessions, I reacted like a human, not as a puppy trainer. I ooh'd and ah'd and cooed and fussed over the puppy — and then winced as the barking split my eardrums. Oops. You see, the puppy was absolutely gorgeous, and I'll admit I was blindsided by how he looked. But his behaviour was not cute, and I had a job to do.

Over several months we worked together to teach the puppy quieter, alternative behaviours to replace his banshee-like barking, which he no longer does. If we hadn't worked together on positively and gently teaching the puppy that he didn't need to lose his shit every time someone walked through the door, nothing would have changed, and the barking would have continued past puppyhood and into adulthood.

He's only a puppy... a people problem

When I started venturing out into the world as a puppy trainer, a couple of phrases would literally boil my piss. The first was, "Oh, I don't mind if your puppy does that." And the second was, "He's only a puppy." Often these irritating sentences, which I still hear frequently, are uttered by members of the general public. The conversation will usually go like this:

> MoP: Ooh, is that a puppy? Ooh, can I say hello then? *whilst already sticking their hands into the puppy's face*
>
> Me: No, sorry, the puppy is in training; we're teaching him not to jump up at strangers.
>
> MoP: *edging ever closer as puppy rears onto their back legs* Ooh, I don't mind! He's very cute!
>
> Puppy: Hey, this person doesn't mind if I jump all over them; I like this person.

Me: Sorry, but we need to be getting on with our training; you're confusing the puppy by letting him jump up at you.

My client: *shifts around awkwardly*

MoP: How old is he? Isn't he cute, is he allowed a treat? *whilst fishing in their pockets*

Me: No, sorry, he's not allowed a treat right now; as I said, we're in training, and you're not helping.

MoP: Well, there's no need to be rude; I was only saying hello.

Often I'll joke (even though I'm usually being serious about it) that the worst part of my job is dealing with the public. Their skills include an innate ability to scupper your training efforts with your puppy by letting them practise the same behaviours you really want to stop. In turn, this reinforces your puppy's choices, causes confusion and makes your job much harder. Sadly, you are not alone in experiencing this; none of us are immune to it. This happens a lot when it comes to encounters between your puppy and strangers.

Stranger Danger

If you think I'm just scaremongering, exaggerating, or being ridiculous, let me tell you the story of a lady called Pauline Wilson. Pauline was mum to a French bulldog puppy called Jimmy, who was as cute as a button at just ten months old. Sadly, his good looks didn't stop him from landing Pauline with a suspended jail sentence. What was Jimmy's crime? What damage could a ten-month-old Frenchie possibly do that would warrant a suspended jail sentence? Well, I hope you're sitting down. Jimmy, whilst on a lead and supposedly under Pauline's control, began to get over-excited during a walk, to the extent that he jumped up at two members of the public.

In the first instance, he scratched a lady's arm as she tried to fend him off; and later he caused bruising to another person as they tried to get him to stop jumping up at them. Jimmy was reported as behaving dangerously out of control, and Pauline was taken to court. The judge ruled that Jimmy was not, in fact, a dangerous dog, but in order to protect the public, he would have to be muzzled at all times outside of his home. He would no longer be allowed to be walked by anyone under the age of sixteen. And he must be crated whenever people visit his home. All that just because he jumped up? I'm afraid so. I'm sharing this story because Pauline's defence included the dreaded words: "He's only a puppy."

In the UK, a puppy can be considered dangerously out of control for behaviours such as jumping at strangers, chasing them, or rushing up to strangers. The defence that "he's only a puppy" won't help you, and it definitely didn't help Jimmy or Pauline. Think about this the next time you're feeling embarrassed or awkward about saying no to a well-meaning stranger who wants to pet your puppy, unless you're absolutely sure your puppy isn't going to jump up at them. You are the guardian of your puppy, and you shouldn't feel pressured into letting other people, or kids, invade your pup's space. Stick up for your puppy, and if you don't like what's happening, get yourself, and your pup, the heck out of there.

Do No Harm, but Take No Shit

There have been many times during my outdoor puppy training sessions when I've had to implement the same things I've just shared with you, particularly when members of the public have unhelpfully tried to help, whilst proving they have absolutely no idea about why puppies behave the way they do.

I've been told I should be throwing a slip lead around the puppy's neck and applying pressure — handling the puppy like a puppet on some very painful strings. For the puppies that pull, I've been told to buy a head collar, which tightly pinches the puppy's face whenever they stop walking to heel. Each time I've been very blunt with the offending member of the public and then calmly explained to my client why we will not be doing these very stupid things. You see, the public does not know your puppy better than you do, and the public will not have your puppy's best interests at heart in the way that you do, or your trainer does.

As difficult as it may be, I strongly urge you not to be swayed or influenced by the public's opinion of what they think you should be doing. Don't be afraid to stick up for your puppy or to stick two fingers up at any shitty advice you might be given. There is no science to this approach — all you need to do is trust yourself and your gut instinct. If you're making good progress by following positive, kind and gentle training techniques, why would you believe you need to adopt a much heavier-handed approach? Did you bring your puppy home with the intention of hurting them? Didn't think so.

As I said earlier, puppies rarely grow out of the behaviours you don't like. All that happens is they get to practice the same things over and over again, until it becomes a problem — your problem. When, and if, you do eventually reach out to a force-free puppy trainer, it will take a lot longer to resolve the puppy problems. This is not your trainer's fault, it simply means your puppy has had lots of time to practice the behaviours you don't like, and they now need to unlearn those particular habits.

Finding the balance between meeting your puppy's emotional and physical needs, whilst setting them up for a successful life, isn't always easy. It can be a struggle to decide what to prioritise and what to leave for later. The way I think about this is: "Does my puppy need to know how to do this right now, or is it just something that I want them to do?" Consider this the next time your puppy does something you don't like.

Before I talk you through what happens next, I'd like you to start trusting yourself more. Have confidence in your instincts, faith in your gut instinct. If you don't feel comfortable doing something to your puppy in the name of training, just don't do it. If what you're doing is working well, but other people are making you feel insecure or worried about it, ask me for help. Don't Google, don't ask your neighbours or the lady in the supermarket who had a dog thirty years ago — it will likely only make you feel worse. There is absolutely no reason why you can't raise, train and socialise your puppy to be practically perfect (not a lie).

What Happens Next?

What happens next is completely up to you. I'm not being sarcastic – it's true! You are your puppy's guardian. Their champion. Their hero. You, owner of opposable thumbs, have the power to take on as much, or as little, of this book as you want.

If anything, I'd like you to have a little moment to think about why you picked this book up, what was it that made you think, "Ooh this looks interesting," and what prompted you to keep reading until the end? Do you feel differently about your puppy, now you've read it?

I wrote this book because I wanted to talk to you about the things that no-one else is. I wanted you to feel empowered, calm and confident when it came to raising, training and socialising your puppy.

To be honest, I was scared when I wrote this book. As I was writing, I remember one of my best friends (hi Anna) who has grown up with dogs for most of her life, and is a fountain of doggy knowledge asking me how I knew the difference between good and bad training advice. Nobody had ever asked me that before, and I'll admit that her question caught me off guard. I tried to answer in a clever, professional and technical way, and failed miserably. Because the answer isn't about being clever, professional or technical. It's actually about gut instinct.

Your gut instinct.

If there's only one thing you take away from this book, I hope it's to trust your instinct. Your natural reaction to being told what to do with your puppy, how to train them, how to raise them. Especially if you're still feeling a little bit bewildered, confused, or conflicted by the masses of training "advice" that's roaming freely and often dangerously. Trust your gut instinct, and if you don't trust it, ask yourself:

- How does this training advice make me feel?
- Is this something that's going to hurt my puppy?
- Do I feel comfortable doing this thing to my puppy?
- Does my puppy need to know how to do this?
- Can I be arsed training this?

And that's it. We don't need to overcomplicate ourselves with technical training theories and techniques. We often just want to know how to stop the puppy behaviour we don't like.

In my case, I wanted to know how to stop G from constantly toileting in the house. I wanted to fix her separation anxiety. Stop her from nipping other dogs on the bum during play, or chasing after on-lead dogs (yes, I was that terrible owner who couldn't always control my dog). To know how to manage her extreme travel sickness (from both ends). I wanted to teach her house manners and feel confident that she would come back when we called her – instead of watching her leg it in the opposite direction.

I wanted to be sure the training techniques I was following weren't harmful, painful or dangerous. If you can set your criteria accordingly, and remember to enjoy your relationship with your puppy, you'll find it so much easier to filter everyone else's voices out, and most importantly, to trust and have confidence in your own.

If you've loved this book

If you've loved this book, there's three things you can do.

The first is to write a review.

Reviews are really helpful to me, and they help me to help more puppy owners.

If you could write a review sharing what you liked about the book, and how it's helped you and your puppy, that would be absolutely fantastic!

Please leave me a Google review by typing Meera Puppins into Google, and then clicking on the "review" tab. I won't include a direct link, because we all know how quickly technology changes.

If you're struggling with a Google review, please email your review to me instead, to:

meerapuppins@gmail.com

The second thing is to tell your friends and family about this book, or maybe even buy them a copy!

The third is if you've enjoyed my approach to puppy training, and you'd like to work with me, please head over to my website and get in touch with me at www.meerapuppins.co.uk.

Through the Contact page of my website you can book a free 15-minute discovery call with me, where we can have a chat about the puppy problems you're struggling with, and how I can help you.

If there's something else you'd like to talk about, you can always ping me an email to meerapuppins@gmail.com.

Acknowledgements

People who deserve to be mentioned in this book — even if it is only at the end

My dad. For taking me to the library as soon as I was old enough to read, and for paying all of my overdue book fines.

My mum. For taking me to the opticians to get my first pair of reading glasses, and for not accusing me of reading too much.

My friends. For still believing that I will leave the house to have fun with you, instead of working and writing all of the time.

Simon. You deserve a mention because I've been an absolute goblin whilst writing this book.

Tig Tay George. For the moral support, the insightful chats, and your friendship. And also for helping to make Chapter 1 about puppies, and not about the other thing.

Gemma & Steve Lea. For helpfully and honestly reading the shitty first draft, and for your feedback, which has made this book a lot less shitty.

Dominic Hodgson. Surprise! I wrote a book! Thank you for gently and supportively scaring the absolute crap out of me at every wibbly wobbly step of building Meera Puppins.

Vicky Quinn Fraser. For your Tiny Beetle Steps — and everything else.

My puppy training & socialisation clients, past, present and future. Thank you for trusting me with your puppy, and for letting me be a part of your incredible journey.

P.S. I am absolutely awful at ending things in a good way, so I'll just awkwardly say bye, and hope that you're feeling a bit sad to have reached the end of this book.

I'd also like to remind you of the practical things you can do on the "If you Loved this Book" page (I don't know what the page number is, sorry, because I don't understand how book formatting stuff works).

P.P.S. I did warn you I am terrible at ending things in a good way *awkwardly waves goodbye*

Ingram Content Group UK Ltd.
Milton Keynes UK
UKHW012133140323
418576UK00001B/78

9 781399 943635